Blessed
is the Spot

Words by Bahá'u'lláh

Illustrations by Constanze von Kitzing

BELLWOOD
PRESS

Bellwood Press
401 Greenleaf Avenue, Wilmette, Illinois 60091
Copyright © 2013 by the
National Spiritual Assembly of the
Bahá'ís of the United States

22 21 20 19   4 3 2

Library of Congress
Bahá'u'lláh, 1817–1892.
  [Prayers. Selections. English.]
  Blessed is the spot / words by Bahá'u'lláh ; illustrations by Constanze Von Kitzing.
    pages cm
  ISBN 978-1-61851-048-8 (alk. paper)
 1. Bahai children—Prayers and devotions. I. Von Kitzing, Constanze, illustrator. II. Title.
  BP362.A3 2013b
  297.9'3433—dc23
                        2013016867

Book design by Patrick Falso
Illustrations by Constanze von Kitzing

For my parents

Blessed is the spot,

and the house,

and the place,

and the city,

and the heart,

and the mountain,

and the refuge,

and the cave,

and the valley,

and the land,

and the sea,

and the island,

and the meadow

where mention of God
hath been made,
and His praise glorified.